Scholar of the Arts and Inhumanities

poems by

Rebecca Dietrich

Finishing Line Press
Georgetown, Kentucky

Scholar of the Arts and Inhumanities

ACKNOWLEDGMENTS

"Chokehold," Poets Choice, *Injured – Words Are Sharper Than A Sword*
"Reclaim," *Plumwood Mountain Journal, A Poetics of Rights*
"Ocean Waves," Wingless Dreamer Publisher, *Sea or Seashore*
"Unfair," Ludington Writers, *Making Waves: A West Michigan Review*
"Ghost," Black Spot Books, *Under Her Eye*

Publisher: Leah Huete de Maines
Editor: Christen Kincaid
Cover Art: Rebecca Dietrich
Author Photo: Rebecca Dietrich
Cover Design: Elizabeth Maines McCleavy

Order online: www.finishinglinepress.com
also available on amazon.com

Author inquiries and mail orders:
Finishing Line Press
PO Box 1626
Georgetown, Kentucky 40324
USA

Table of Contents

*This book is dedicated to the man who turned
inhumanity into an art form.
I would like to thank Liz for putting up with my craziness on a
regular basis. You are not a therapist, but I feel like
I should pay you by the hour anyway.
Amber, for supporting all my decisions, even the bad ones.
Amina, I know I promised you my first born but I hope this
acknowledgement will suffice in the meantime.
Elana, you are the best Big a sorority sister could ask for.
Please move back to New Jersey.
Jon, thank you for being a true friend and proving not all men suck.*

Sinking

I wished for a love
I would always remember
But I feel myself sinking
Below the surface
Of an ocean I christened
With my own tears
You taught me
That wishes can come true
Just not the way I expected

Canary

My sweet canary
My world was silent
Before you sang to me
I was a naive child
Now I know the truth
Your melancholy song
Brought me to tears
Do not feel ashamed
I needed to hear it
Thank you

Vengeful Spirit

You throw my lifeless body
Into the trunk of your car
I hope keeping your little secret
Was worth my short life
Can you really pretend
That your actions won't haunt you
I may no longer feel
The potholes you run over
But my soul lingers on
Fed by vengeance and regret
I am the spirit of all women wronged
You cannot bury me

Trauma Bond

I have always seen you as you are
Both the good and the evil within
And I have loved you just the same
Even when you hurt me and others too
I broke free from our relationship
But not the chains placed on my psyche
The voice inside me screams for freedom
Yet, I find myself running back to you
This trauma bond we share reels me back
Every time... every time...

Lockdown

Maybe we should have politicians
Practice lockdown drills
Every month
And experience the terror
That our children
Have become numb to
Maybe then
Something will be done

Pink

Canisters of pepper spray
For sale
At a college bookstore
Pink
For breast cancer awareness
Because now you can feel
Safe and feminine
For a good cause

Unfair

We asked for
A seat at the table
So, when they refused
We built our own
Now they claim
That it's unfair
To not be included

Reclaim

They will never
Willingly give up
What they stole
From all of us
We must claim
What belongs to us
Make it their problem
Not ours

Chokehold

Even now I feel your hand
Wrapped around my neck
It would have been easier
If you had squeezed harder
My pale lifeless frame
Hanging by your fingers
Yet here I am
Haunted by your words
What you did and didn't say
My psyche in your grasp
Crushed under the weight
Of what you withheld from me
As I beg for you to let go
I don't know why
You have this hold on me
Let go of me my love

Until We Kiss Again

The last time we kissed
Was December 2019
Not long after Christmas
Your warm touch
Against my cold skin
Sunlight glistened
Off the fresh snow
You told me you hoped
That this kiss would last
Until we meet again
Little did we know
What was on the horizon
That a plague
Would ravage our world
We hid in separate homes
Hoping the end was near
Weeks turned into months
And months into a year
Yet we still had hope
That we may kiss again

The Tears You Gave Me

It has been a year and here I am in therapy
Still trying to figure out what is the truth and what is a lie
But I see you are wearing your wedding ring now
Solid gold and tight around your chubby finger
Without a single tan line to be found underneath
Does she even know what you have done to me?
While you pretend to be a happy family man
You robbed me of my sleep and so much more
Give me back the pieces of me I used to heal you
I was so young and thought the world of you
I kept your secrets and defended you to everyone
I gave you my word and you gave me heartache in return
But you knew the whole time, didn't you?
The tears you gave me taint my happiest memories
And I still have no idea how I survived until now
I do not care how lonely you claim to be
You should have been the one to set me free
I made the hardest choice, though I know it was right
We said goodbye and you never saw me cry
Now I am trying to figure out who I am without you
I hope your heart shatters whenever you hear my name
You owe that much to me and my sanity

You

You are the best secret I ever told
My once happiest memories
Are wrapped in the tears you gave me
I am stronger than the promises you never kept
I don't need your approval anymore
I have always been good enough to be loved

Ocean Waves

I walk into the ocean
And I see the wave
Instead of running away
I face my fears head on
I cannot stop the tide
From coming in
So instead, I wait
For it to pass over me
I do not fear drowning
Only that I might
For the anticipation
Is far worse than reality

Indelible Mark

I try to scrape off
The unholy baptism
You gave me
But you left
An indelible mark
Upon my soul
As my skin bleeds
From trying to remove
With my fingernails
Where you touched me

Thief

I am not a writer
I am a thief
I steal snapshots
Of people's lives
And put them on paper
I snatched your kiss
Only to write it down
Between lines
Of notebook paper
You often wonder
What is my creation
And what is inspiration
How much is real
In my surreal world
Is that you on the page
With a mischievous grin
Winking back at you
Or just a coincidence
Not even I
Know the difference

Victim Blaming

"He would never"
"That's just the way he is"
"He didn't mean it"
"That just means he likes you"
"Why didn't you go to the police"
"You're overreacting"
"Did you tell him to stop"
"You should have just taken it"
"He didn't know any better"
"You should have known better"

Maiden Name

Dietrich
Ruler of the people
My borrowed name
On loan from my father
I felt no allegiance
To my birth name
For I was taught
My permanent name
(Still a mystery)
Will be given to me
By a different man
My mother taught me
A woman has no name
Her identity
Comes from others
Daughter to her father
Wife to her husband
Mother to her sons
From maidenhood to motherhood
A woman is never her own
That changes today

Ghost

Your ghost haunts me
Even though
I'm the one who left
The rattle of the chains
You placed on my heart
Echoes in the night
I still see your face
With that deceiving grin
In my nightmares
Your lingering spirit
Lives on in my mind
Rest In Peace
For I am not

Teacher's Pet

We shared a love of learning
And so much more than that
I was your teacher's pet
Waiting by your desk after class
The hardest lesson I had to learn
Was not part of your syllabus
You opened my heart
When you opened your mouth
My innocence was shattered
Thanks to your devilish grin
I did not stand a chance
Against your tempting glance
I was so young, so full of life
Were you hoping to take some for yourself?
I was happy to give my all to you
But that did not cure your sickness
The truth awoken me one night
And I have yet to sleep
My knight-errant, my Byronic hero
You were supposed to rescue me
Not lead me to my grave

Pieces of Me

You consumed my life
For the past five years
I just want to know
Who I am
And not who you
Wanted me to be
Give me back
The pieces of me
I gave you
To heal your broken heart

Rebecca Dietrich is a writer and genocide scholar from the Jersey Shore. Her poetry has been featured in publications such as *Plumwood Mountain Journal, Making Waves: A West Michigan Review,* and *Black Spot Books.* Dietrich holds a B.A. in Psychology from Stockton University.